Things to Do While You Poop

Activity Book For Adults

Table of Contents

1. What is Bob Dylan's real name?

    A. Lind Zimmerman
    B. Robert Zimmerman
    C. Adam Zimmerman
    D. Jonathan Zimmerman

2. Johnny Depp is famously afraid of what?

    A. Tarantulas
    B. Thunder
    C. Clowns
    D. Elevators

3. Caesar salad originated from which country?

    A. Italy
    B. Mexico
    C. France
    D. Italy

4. Who wrote Flowers for Algernon?

    A. Herman Hesse
    B. Philip Roth
    C. Daniel Keyes
    D. Ira Levin

5. What did Spain introduce to Ireland in the late 1500s?

    A. Corn
    B. Potatoes
    C. Tomatoes
    D. Beans

6. Which famous landmark is visible from space?

    A. The Great Wall of China
    B. Taj Mahal
    C. The Great Pyramids at Giza
    D. Taipei 101

7. What is the smallest country in the world?

    A. Monaco
    B. Liechtensttein
    C. Malta
    D. Vatican City

8. In 1917 Finland declared its independence from which country?

    A. Sweden
    B. Norway
    C. Denmark
    D. Russia

9. The Paris Peace Accords ended which conflict?

A. WWI
B. WWII
C. Vietnam War
D. Korean War

10. Which country is the least populated?

A. Vatican City
B. Palau
C. Monaco
D. San Marino

11. What is the main ingredient of Bombay Duck?

A. Swan
B. Chicken
C. Pork
D. Fish

12. DNA is arranged into structures known as what?

A. amino acids
B. chromosomes
C. mitochondria
D. RNA

13. Which city was Beethoven born in?

    A. Bonn
    B. Berlin
    C. Munich
    D. Warsaw

14. What is the only king in a deck of cards without a moustache?

    A. King of spades
    B. King of hearts
    C. King of diamonds
    D. King of clubs

15. Where might you keep bees?

    A. apiary
    B. aquarium
    C. aviary
    D. vivarium

16. In what year did Neil Armstrong land on the moon?

    A. 1966
    B. 1967
    C. 1968
    D. 1969

17. What year did Queen Victoria become Queen?

    A. 1845

    B. 1829

    C. 1835

    D. 1837

18. What happened in the Soviet Union from 1933-1934?

    A. Famine

    B. War

    C. Uprising

    D. Political conflicts

19. What is the capital of Qatar?

    A. Dukhan

    B. Doha

    C. Abu Dhabi

    D. Dubai

20. What year did Harriet Tubman escape slavery?

    A. 1850

    B. 1845

    C. 1849

    D. 1840

21. Marilyn Monroe was married to which famous sportsman?

    A. Yogi Berra
    B. Justin Verlander
    C. Ralph Kiner
    D. Joe DiMaggio

22. Which New York Yankee player was nicknamed the "Yankee Clipper"?

    A. Joe DiMaggio
    B. Mickey Mantle
    C. Whitey Ford
    D. Roger Maris

23. Which gas makes up 91% of the sun?

    A. helium
    B. hydrogen
    C. nitrogen
    D. oxygen

24. What is the longest mountain range in the world?

    A. Alaska Range
    B. Andes
    C. Himalayas
    D. Tian Shan

25. Which instrument is associated with Earl Bud Powell?

A. Bass
B. Guitar
C. Flute
D. Piano

26. What christian denomination was founded by John Wesley in 1738?

A. Methodist
B. Anabaptist
C. Episcopalianism
D. Pentecostal

27. In what month does Russia celebrate the October Revolution?

A. November
B. December
C. September
D. October

28. Which US city is known as the City of Brotherly

A. Philadelphia
B. Dallas
C. Chicago
D. Boston

29. Which country is the oldest?

A. Portugal
B. New Zealand
C. Indonesia
D. Australia

30. Which country produces the most coffee in the world?

A. Colombia
B. Vietnam
C. Mexico
D. Brazil

31. Julius Caesar was kidnapped by who in 78 BC?

A. Senate
B. pirates
C. enemy nation
D. family

32. How old was King Tut when he died?

A. 18
B. 16
C. 17
D. 19

33. In June in Wyoming it is illegal to take a picture of what?

    A. An elk
    B. A bison
    C. A geyser
    D. A rabbit

34. Where did Rene Descartes spend the last year of his life?

    A. France
    B. Belgium
    C. Sweden
    D. Denmark

35. In what country would one compete in a wife carry race?

    A. Sweden
    B. Denmark
    C. Finland
    D. Norway

36. The Ring of Fire is located in which ocean?

    A. Indian
    B. Atlantic
    C. Pacific
    D. Arctic

37. Where is the Easter Island located?

    A. Chile
    B. China
    C. Morocco
    D. Singapore

38. Name the team with the most Super Bowl appearances?

    A. Buffalo Bills
    B. New England Patriots
    C. Dallas Cowboys
    D. Pittsburgh Steelers

39. Which of the following is not a computer coding language?

    A. Java
    B. Python
    C. Ruby
    D. Snake

40. What is the name of Donald Duck's sister?

    A. Dorathy Duck
    B. Della Duck
    C. Daisy Duck
    D. Daphne Duck

41. Which of Shakespeare's plays is the longest?

A. Macbeth
B. The Tempest
C. Hamlet
D. Taming of the Shrew

42. What igneous rock has a density less than water?

A. Basalt
B. Granite
C. Scoria
D. Pumice

43. Which U.S. President was the first to hold a Patent?

A. Washington
B. Adams
C. Jackson
D. Lincoln

44. What does a pteridologist study?

A. dinosaurs
B. ferns
C. mushrooms
D. terrapins

45. Which Dutch artist painted Girl with a Pearl Earring?

A. Rembrandt
B. Mondrian
C. Vermeer
D. Bosch

46. The oldest living person lived in which country?

A. France
B. Japan
C. Italy
D. USA

47. Who was the first tsar of Russia?

A. Ivan IV
B. Peter I
C. Paul I
D. Catherine I

48. How many times was Dr. Seuss's first book rejected?

A. 27
B. 30
C. 1
D. 10

49. What planets literally rain diamonds?

    A. Uranus and Neptune
    B. Mercury and Venus
    C. Saturn and Neptune
    D. Saturn and Jupiter

50. What year did women get the right to vote in the U.S?

    A. 1920
    B. 1919
    C. 1918
    D. 1921

Assorted Words 1

```
S  E  C  O  N  D  H  A  N  D  Z  S  K  N  P
J  P  S  E  R  G  E  U  N  M  W  I  I  D  H
A  O  C  V  K  J  N  S  B  L  U  S  H  E  R
C  X  O  R  B  E  V  I  T  N  E  T  E  R  N
G  N  I  T  A  U  T  C  E  F  F  E  C  I  Q
U  X  F  O  T  S  U  O  N  E  V  A  R  I  B
Z  J  F  J  M  P  B  G  D  Q  C  R  U  K  D
Z  S  I  H  C  A  S  G  N  E  J  M  Z  L  I
L  T  N  S  P  A  T  E  S  I  T  O  E  B  S
E  U  G  I  S  F  E  I  H  C  K  F  I  Z  V
R  M  M  X  E  F  L  I  C  K  E  R  I  N  G
X  P  D  E  H  S  I  D  N  A  R  B  A  R  S
K  I  D  E  Z  E  P  A  R  T  L  C  X  L  G
U  N  A  D  O  R  N  E  D  L  A  L  Q  Q  V
D  G  S  H  I  M  M  I  E  S  F  I  Y  V  H
```

AXIOMATICALLY	FLICKERING	SERGE
BLUSHER	GUZZLER	SHIMMIES
BRANDISHED	JOINS	SPATES
CHIEFS	LARKING	STUMPING
COIFFING	RAVENOUS	TRAPEZED
DICTUM	RETENTIVE	UNADORNED
EFFECTUATING	RIFTED	
EMCEEING	SECONDHAND	

Assorted Words 2

```
P  Y  S  F  R  A  N  C  H  I  S  E  D  C  X
S  E  N  T  Z  C  B  E  S  A  B  E  E  R  F
G  R  N  T  N  A  R  C  H  D  E  A  C  O  N
R  U  E  O  N  E  T  B  Z  V  E  D  F  S  H
S  R  G  U  I  A  M  S  A  E  R  V  Z  S  P
R  N  E  R  S  T  N  Y  I  R  F  O  Y  R  U
F  S  O  S  A  C  U  G  O  E  G  C  P  O  S
M  F  G  I  S  D  E  B  I  L  H  A  T  A  H
Y  U  O  N  S  O  U  R  I  L  P  T  I  D  E
U  M  S  W  I  R  R  A  V  R  A  E  N  N  R
K  B  U  C  O  L  E  C  T  I  T  M  D  A  S
K  L  Q  U  L  H  B  V  H  I  C  T  N  J  P
I  E  P  Y  U  E  S  M  R  W  O  A  A  O  N
N  D  U  L  C  Q  D  H  U  E  A  N  L  D  N
G  S  V  P  I  L  L  S  M  B  P  N  S  B  F
```

ADVOCATE	DEPLOYMENTS	PERVERSIONS
ARCHDEACON	FRANCHISED	PILLS
ATTRIBUTION	FREEBASE	PUSHERS
BARGAINS	FUMBLED	SHOWOFF
BUMBLINGS	GRADUATIONS	SUERS
CERVICAL	MUSCLED	YUKKING
CROSSER	NONMALIGNANT	
CROSSROAD	PANTHEIST	

Assorted Words 3

```
M  J  V  Z  I  R  R  I  G  A  T  E  S  P  S
P  O  V  E  R  D  R  E  S  S  I  N  G  S  P
R  R  L  Y  R  I  C  S  W  C  P  R  B  Y  E
E  E  R  M  U  C  E  U  E  O  G  Y  E  R  E
C  E  Y  E  S  N  A  G  Y  N  L  C  U  I  D
A  L  A  M  F  D  M  M  B  F  I  G  A  R  B
U  I  Z  O  A  Y  A  A  U  I  S  B  Y  U  O
T  N  O  I  T  C  A  R  T  S  I  D  R  N  A
I  G  S  R  I  P  A  T  G  C  N  V  O  A  T
O  F  F  S  P  R  I  N  G  A  H  V  K  W  C
N  N  G  G  K  W  F  L  A  T  B  E  D  A  K
S  S  T  N  E  M  A  M  R  I  F  B  D  Y  R
R  S  T  I  N  T  E  R  P  O  S  E  S  Y  I
K  F  W  I  Y  R  O  T  A  N  I  M  F  W  D
M  O  U  N  T  A  I  N  T  O  P  S  P  L  K
```

CARBINES	IRRIGATES	REELING
CONFISCATION	LYRICS	RUNAWAY
DISTRACTION	MEMOIRS	SPEEDBOAT
FIRMAMENTS	MINATORY	SUMAC
FLATBED	MOUNTAINTOPS	TAPIRS
GLOWER	OFFSPRING	UNMATCHED
GRADS	OVERDRESSING	
INTERPOSES	PRECAUTIONS	

Puzzle #4

Assorted Words 4

```
G  I  T  G  P  Y  H  T  I  W  E  R  E  H  D
W  I  Y  S  N  R  L  O  W  O  S  F  O  Z  M
S  S  M  R  N  I  O  L  N  B  Z  A  S  Z  R
S  A  R  I  A  A  H  F  A  E  S  D  H  G  E
M  S  T  O  S  D  M  C  F  R  S  D  Y  B  D
L  T  E  C  T  S  I  O  T  E  E  T  O  U  U
S  E  O  T  H  A  I  U  T  O  R  D  L  H  C
U  H  A  C  A  E  R  N  S  T  L  E  E  Y  T
T  L  Z  F  E  M  L  R  A  E  O  B  D  F  I
B  O  U  I  L  L  A  B  A  I  S  S  E  R  O
L  I  K  E  N  E  D  G  H  N  P  R  F  Q  N
D  I  P  R  O  T  V  L  L  A  B  T  O  O  F
F  Y  D  S  I  D  I  O  M  A  T  I  C  U  C
E  N  O  Y  V  W  G  N  I  P  M  I  R  C  G
T  R  A  C  H  E  A  S  O  A  C  A  C  J  U
```

AMALGAMATES	HONESTLY	REDUCTION
BLOTCHING	IDIOMATIC	SATCHEL
BOUILLABAISSE	LIKENED	TORPID
CACAOS	NARRATORS	TRACHEAS
CRIMPING	OTTOMANS	
FEDERALLY	PIANISSIMI	
FOOTBALL	PROFFERED	
HEREWITH	RADIUSES	

Assorted Words 5

```
A D M O N I S H M E N T S S Q
V S E Z G E W C L P W B O H S
Z S D N G N O T I C E D L O Q
P E S I N N I C E N G M V V U
E R J G G A I K L Q I I E E E
R V S T L F P N A O N L X L E
S I G A E O E D E M G Z C I Z
U C Z X A L R Y A T H S P N E
A E S I M L M Y V E S C Z G R
S A Q I S I A Y S V D I T Y S
I B U N D E R A R F N I O A H
O L A G A S P S T O K E S M M
N E W P A R B O I L S V K H X
U D S E Z I R A L O P G E A N
H F F H N E M Y R E S R U N Z
```

ADMONISHMENTS	INFRARED	SERVICEABLE
CLINICS	MATCHMAKING	SHOVELING
CLOGS	MOISTENING	SOLVE
DEADPANNED	NOTICED	SQUAWS
ELOPES	NURSERYMEN	SQUEEZERS
FOLLIES	PARBOILS	STOKES
GLEAMS	PERSUASION	TAXIING
GLORY	POLARIZES	

Assorted Words 6

```
Y  S  P  E  L  A  T  A  C  R  E  H  C  N  P
V  N  D  E  V  I  S  U  L  L  I  W  A  Z  E
F  L  O  O  R  E  C  O  R  D  E  D  N  L  R
J  H  U  G  N  I  K  L  I  M  G  Q  N  U  S
Y  U  C  L  A  R  B  I  T  R  A  T  O  R  E
R  J  H  A  O  W  E  Y  P  D  R  D  N  I  V
E  E  I  S  K  O  A  V  L  G  B  O  B  D  E
S  V  N  G  E  J  S  D  B  I  I  G  A  N  R
U  I  G  G  S  R  X  E  I  W  M  F  L  E  A
M  L  S  X  C  A  O  I  N  E  J  O  L  S  N
I  D  L  Y  M  R  W  C  N  S  S  U  O  S  C
N  O  G  A  L  M  A  N  A  C  S  G  E  L  E
G  E  V  B  A  A  Q  G  C  B  R  H  N  L  G
E  R  G  B  Q  Z  N  B  L  T  L  T  W  X  Y
Z  S  Y  F  A  X  P  A  E  K  Z  A  U  B  U
```

AGONY	DOGFOUGHT	LURIDNESS
ALBACORES	DOUCHING	MILKING
ALMANACS	EVILDOERS	PERSEVERANCE
ANALYSIS	FLOOR	RECORDED
ARBITRATOR	GLOOMILY	RESUMING
BINNACLE	ILLUSIVE	WADIES
CANNONBALL	JIGSAW	
CATALEPSY	LOOSENS	

Assorted Words 7

```
K D Q E E S F L O R I D L Y C
U N E C X C U E B E B O I N R
I N M P E O N O Z Q B W M O O
M C F A P L D A U X D F B N S
P U F B U I L E D N E N E P S
E T S E I L R U B R I S R L W
R F R E G R I T L U O T S U A
C W T O P K C N E O N C N S L
E L H P B S Y H G L I K N O K
P R Z J M P I C K E R D I O C
T C O M M E M O R A T E S N C
I S T N E M T S I L N E E B G
B E E S Y O S T E N G A M K L
L S E S S O R T A B L A Z K D
E R E H C N U P W O C S E Y H
```

ALBATROSSES	COWPUNCHER	MAULING
ATTEMPT	CROSSWALK	NONPLUS
BIRCH	DEBUNKING	PICKER
BURLIEST	ENLISTMENTS	TRIPPED
CELLULOID	FLORIDLY	
COMMEMORATES	IMPERCEPTIBLE	
CONCORDANCE	LIMBERS	
CONTINUOUS	MAGNETS	

Assorted Words 8

```
Z  B  X  K  V  M  D  H  O  B  B  L  I  N  G
N  T  D  Q  K  B  D  I  P  O  L  E  V  A  W
X  O  M  E  L  B  M  E  T  S  E  L  B  O  N
M  B  I  P  X  A  S  E  D  E  D  J  C  P  D
E  D  L  T  Y  O  E  G  T  N  O  Q  D  I  G
A  R  M  O  R  S  M  P  N  A  E  F  W  E  E
D  U  Q  Z  O  O  S  M  R  I  M  C  U  L  G
O  E  H  F  Y  D  B  E  U  O  L  I  S  L  D
Y  J  N  H  J  M  S  A  M  L  M  S  T  E  G
B  V  U  E  S  N  M  H  I  Q  F  O  I  L  D
I  I  P  J  E  W  U  K  O  T  L  E  T  U  U
M  S  E  S  U  R  E  V  O  T  N  U  X  E  Q
Y  G  D  U  P  W  A  F  F  U  G  A  N  G  R
G  G  N  I  S  O  L  C  E  R  O  F  R  X  Y
C  M  F  R  A  N  C  H  I  S  E  E  S  U  H
```

ANTIABORTION	FOETID	PROMOTER
ARMORS	FORECLOSING	PUDGY
BLOODSHOT	FRANCHISEES	QUISLINGS
CAREENED	GUFFAW	ULTIMATE
DESCENDED	HOBBLING	
DIPOLE	MESSY	
EMBLEM	NOBLEST	
FLUMMOXED	OVERUSES	

Assorted Words 9

```
G  Y  W  K  D  M  O  O  T  I  N  G  J  R  J
H  M  L  J  P  E  A  I  T  O  I  L  I  N  G
V  V  H  E  H  J  T  S  T  R  A  P  M  A  R
S  Y  Q  F  T  E  X  A  C  T  I  T  U  D  E
D  F  O  N  D  A  N  T  L  E  F  D  W  N  T
F  I  J  G  O  N  R  W  G  U  N  X  X  N  T
O  V  S  G  L  U  I  E  S  T  M  D  K  O  D
R  S  C  C  L  C  Q  C  P  D  Z  U  I  H  B
T  I  A  I  L  M  E  O  I  S  C  U  C  N  U
H  L  Y  S  P  O  O  L  B  T  E  P  F  C  G
W  V  L  J  D  O  S  L  S  R  E  D  I  V  A
I  E  S  S  E  L  T  U  G  H  R  S  A  M  K
T  R  P  U  M  P  E  D  R  I  O  V  D  G  K
H  Y  J  R  E  T  S  E  P  E  W  O  V  J  K
G  E  X  T  R  A  C  T  O  R  S  B  N  P  U
```

ACCUMULATED	EXTRACTOR	RAMPARTS
ASCENDING	FONDANT	SHOON
AVIDER	FORTHWITH	SILVERY
CITES	GLUIEST	TOILING
COLLUDE	GUTLESS	TOPIC
DESPERATELY	MOOTING	
DISCLOSURES	PESTER	
EXACTITUDE	PUMPED	

Assorted Words 10

```
D F T S N O I T A N A L P X E
P C K N O B S I S L L I P S A
X T V D E C S C C E W J W X A
M D S E Z L G L O Y T W D N L
K I E E M V A I U D B T Y U S
G P S N I Z D V T A K G A T G
I N E D J K F A I N Q U I R Y
N R I N I I L D N B D M P I C
N O O Y A R Y I G V M V R T O
Y E I O A C E P M N T A E I N
J U M T M L I C U R N S P O C
A Y N I A I P R T C S I A N O
P K L V G L N T R I C Y R I R
X I A H I E B G U U O O E S D
T A N G I E R O M O H N D T J
```

AMBIVALENT	MILKIEST	ROOMING
ATTEST	MISDIRECTION	SCOUTING
CONCORD	NUTRITIONIST	SPILLS
EXPLANATIONS	OBLATION	TANGIER
GADFLY	OCCUPY	
HURRICANE	OUTPLAYING	
INQUIRY	PREPARED	
KNOBS	REGIMEN	

Maze #1

Maze #2

Maze #3

Maze #4

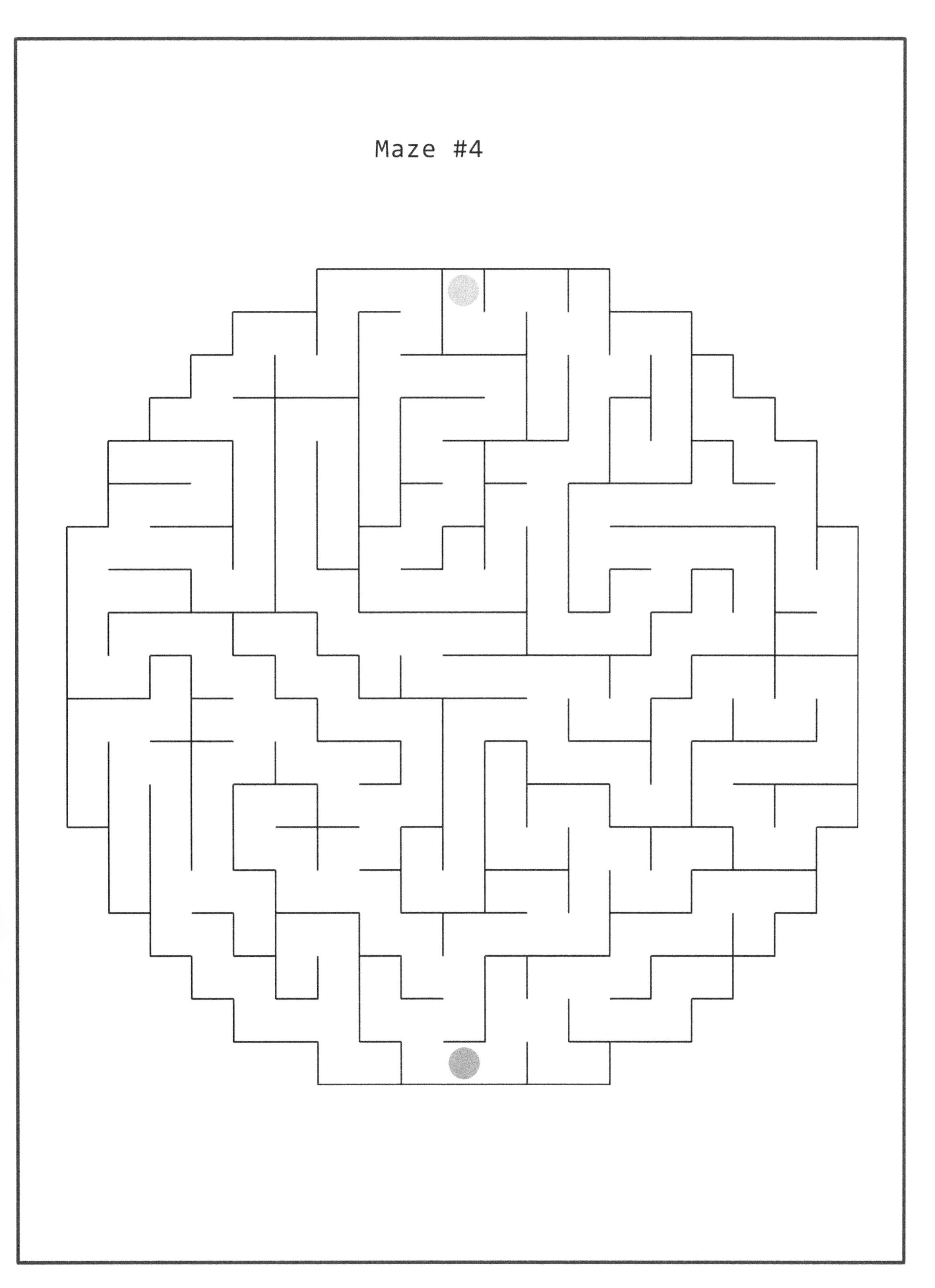

Maze #5

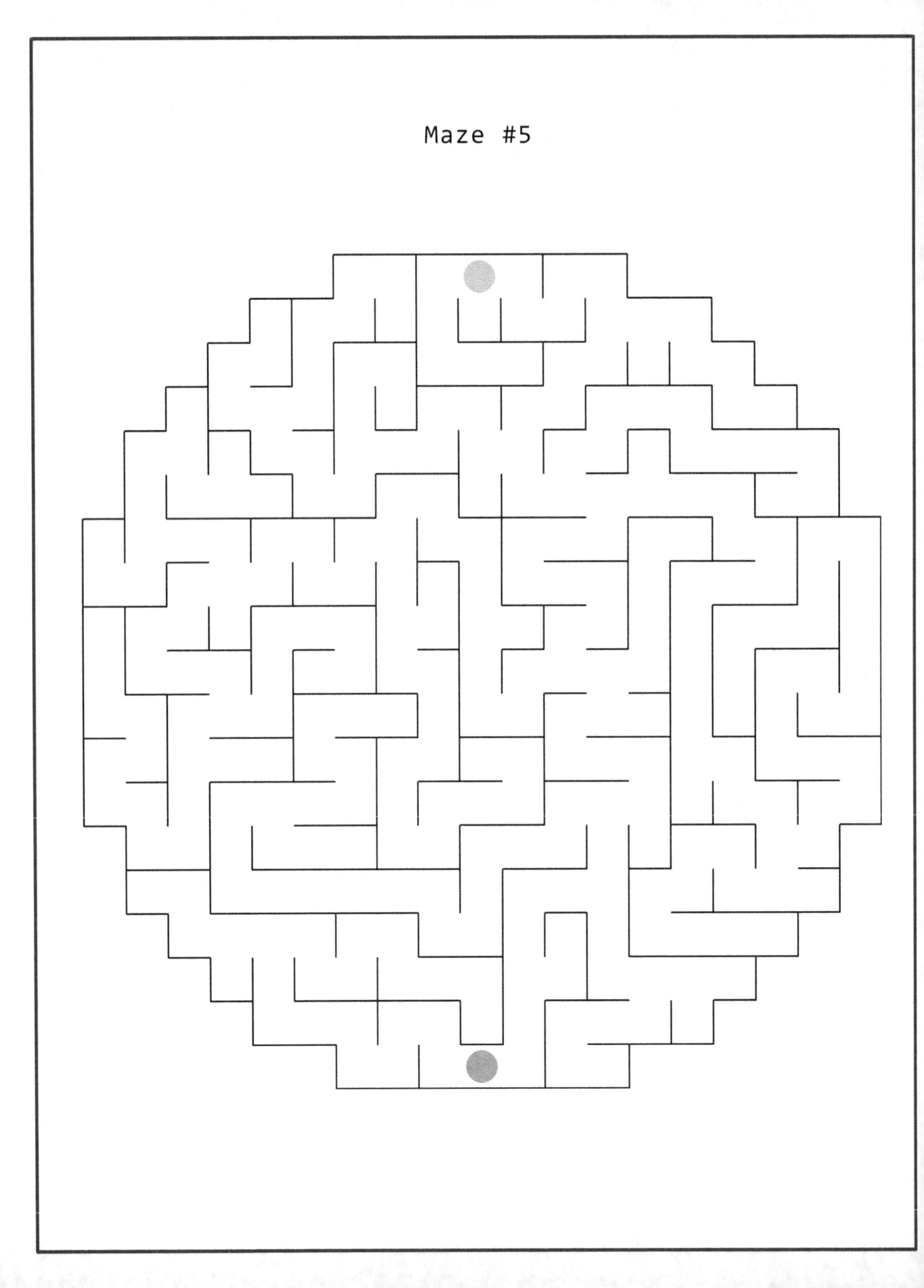

Maze #6

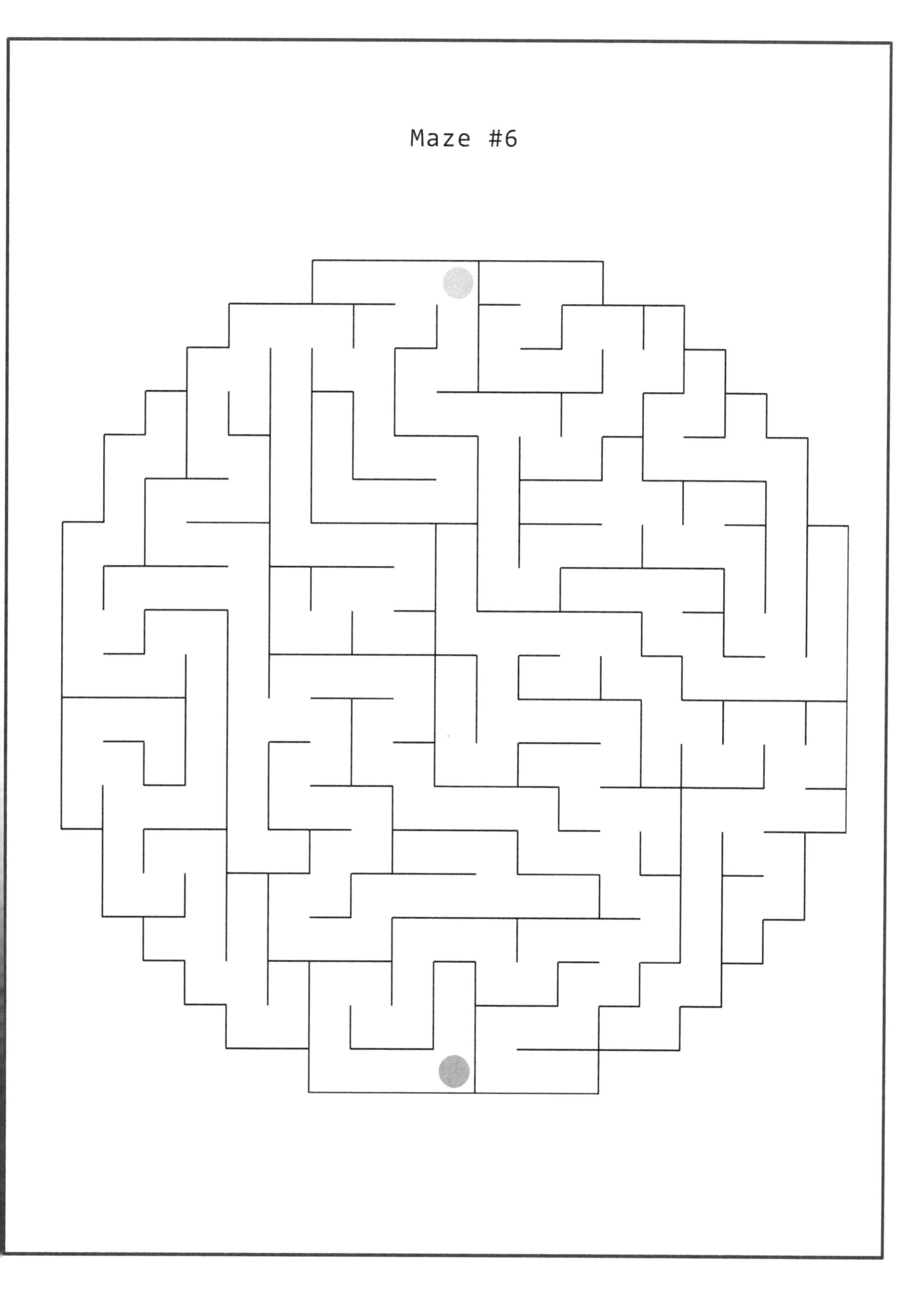

Maze #7

Maze #8

Maze #9

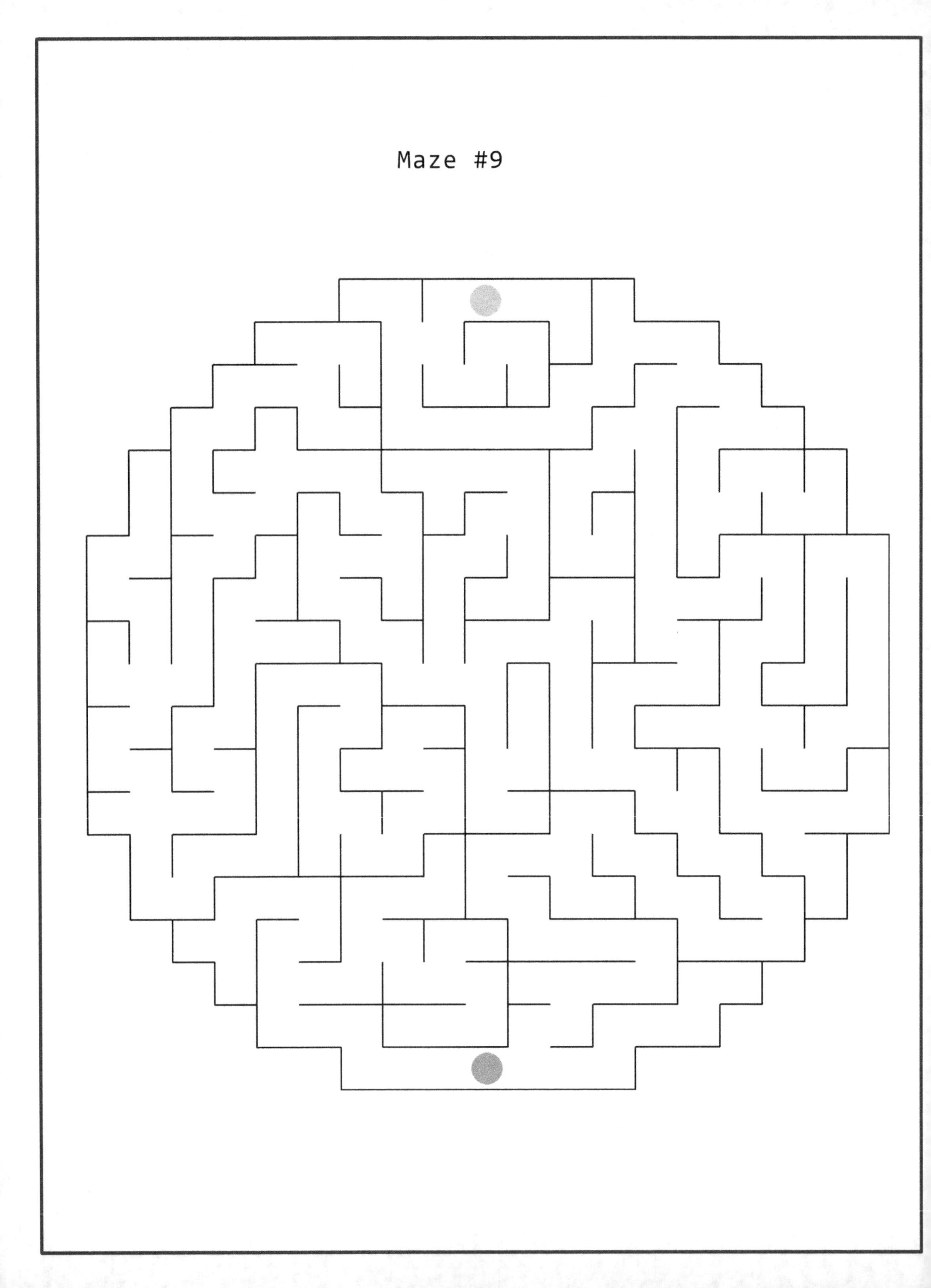

Maze #10

Puzzle #1

FIND THE NUMBERS

```
9  4  3  8  1  8  9  9  1  4  7  4  2  0  8
6  0  3  6  8  5  3  2  8  7  3  4  1  7  3
3  0  0  0  3  0  2  1  5  8  4  7  7  4  3
2  4  3  3  1  8  0  3  4  9  0  1  2  9  8
3  4  9  7  3  0  8  4  3  2  1  1  4  2  0
4  8  3  8  4  0  1  3  3  8  3  4  2  3  3
3  3  8  4  4  2  5  0  0  0  9  8  4  7  0
7  5  8  0  8  1  3  4  4  1  9  8  1  2  5
4  7  3  4  8  0  7  4  1  5  1  4  0  8  4
3  4  4  4  2  1  2  0  2  8  4  4  2  0  1
4  4  5  1  3  8  2  0  7  0  8  2  1  1  8
1  3  0  2  4  1  4  0  9  2  9  6  0  4  8
0  8  8  6  6  3  4  3  1  0  4  3  8  2  1
1  3  9  3  8  2  0  7  8  4  3  2  8  9  4
0  9  4  5  5  4  7  8  4  3  2  8  9  4  7
```

008983	903400	2078432894
14884	1038836	2707148943
34147	1832413	833803054188
50894	5744383	9455478432894
80142	9020843	
0101034	24102108	
148943	24102180	
584774	033054188	
741430	74341010	

FIND THE NUMBERS

2 0 3 4 8 9 0 2 2 0 1 5 3 8 7
0 5 5 4 1 1 8 5 1 8 3 9 5 8 8
7 3 8 9 0 2 1 4 2 7 4 1 3 2 2
2 4 2 2 3 3 8 1 7 5 8 8 2 0 4
0 0 1 7 2 0 1 9 5 2 0 0 0 3 3
3 7 3 4 8 0 9 1 8 3 9 3 7 7 5
2 4 9 8 5 1 3 2 5 9 6 0 4 2 7
1 1 1 3 5 0 3 4 4 8 2 2 7 8 8
1 4 1 4 7 5 6 1 1 5 3 7 7 2 3
7 6 0 3 2 8 8 8 8 4 3 7 4 3 6
1 4 3 9 0 4 8 4 0 7 6 8 8 8 7
9 3 0 1 8 4 0 0 3 7 9 4 8 8 2
0 8 4 7 8 0 7 2 1 4 4 7 2 8 5
6 5 9 9 1 2 5 9 0 3 1 0 2 1 3
0 3 4 5 0 7 4 7 9 4 8 8 4 7 5

54147
851839
1103049
27092748
032888843

89892748
340741464
2744127087
2781318797
8220341464

388835429039
835102209843
5748849747054

FIND THE NUMBERS

```
4  3  6  5  1  1  8  7  6  8  3  7  1  6  5
4  2  1  0  3  7  4  1  4  3  1  4  4  2  5
6  0  6  3  8  3  4  4  5  1  8  0  5  5  3
8  5  8  8  5  3  1  2  1  1  8  9  9  1  4
5  1  6  1  4  8  4  2  4  5  4  3  8  2  4
4  5  2  3  1  0  0  1  0  8  5  2  6  4  6
8  2  0  0  7  1  0  0  3  2  1  4  0  9  7
1  2  1  4  1  8  4  1  8  3  6  8  3  0  8
8  7  0  7  4  4  3  7  3  3  7  1  3  3  1
7  9  2  5  6  7  5  0  6  6  3  1  4  6  4
4  9  5  2  8  7  0  5  3  0  0  4  7  6  7
9  5  5  9  2  4  6  2  7  8  4  9  8  3  8
9  9  4  3  3  4  7  3  4  8  8  7  1  9  3
9  2  4  1  1  4  4  5  1  8  4  3  7  2  4
7  9  5  9  0  7  8  5  9  9  6  2  6  9  5
```

10218	544114	5443836
14842	741836	7489836
37830	781478	9774067
51420	801847	141841836
87074	0833489	742481836
147301	842074	9433473488
189914	1403836	

FIND THE NUMBERS

6	4	0	7	0	0	2	7	0	2	0	7	4	5	0
3	8	8	8	0	3	0	0	0	7	1	0	2	9	0
8	7	3	2	3	1	0	9	7	8	0	7	0	0	4
9	3	0	9	1	0	7	2	2	0	1	0	1	0	6
5	4	4	8	1	3	2	4	3	3	8	0	1	0	0
0	5	0	3	0	0	7	3	0	7	2	6	0	4	2
2	9	0	2	1	9	0	2	0	8	3	0	2	4	7
3	4	7	7	7	9	4	3	4	2	0	3	0	1	8
0	8	0	4	6	0	0	3	0	2	7	0	1	7	2
2	0	0	1	2	8	0	2	2	0	7	0	8	0	2
1	8	7	2	3	8	0	7	0	2	5	3	0	3	7
2	7	2	0	5	7	0	0	8	3	9	0	1	0	0
3	7	0	1	0	6	7	4	2	3	0	4	2	1	3
3	2	7	9	4	3	0	1	0	7	0	2	5	0	0
1	0	2	3	4	2	3	0	2	0	0	2	0	0	6

07203	0720086	00203243201
08883	01083342	0727040000
27002	4027007	070027020745
30243	7030100	101022701903
075027	07203203	
102018	8950230	
400700	20170003	
0701034	27822703	
703700	070832781	

FIND THE NUMBERS

2	4	5	5	0	3	8	3	4	8	6	3	8	2	4
3	4	8	8	8	8	2	7	4	9	3	8	2	6	5
3	7	4	7	5	0	7	6	4	4	7	4	7	2	4
3	9	4	6	4	1	0	0	0	4	7	1	1	7	3
6	9	7	4	0	2	3	0	4	7	1	3	8	8	8
5	4	7	3	5	9	2	9	2	2	2	1	6	9	3
1	8	9	0	5	3	8	7	3	0	5	4	7	8	6
0	0	4	1	1	9	5	0	4	4	7	5	9	2	3
4	2	2	2	0	8	2	2	2	9	7	3	8	8	8
1	3	0	8	0	1	9	0	4	0	2	4	4	7	6
8	0	8	0	8	9	2	5	9	3	1	4	2	3	7
1	4	7	1	4	0	8	4	8	2	4	4	7	3	9
1	3	4	9	1	0	2	4	3	7	0	2	8	8	4
0	8	7	4	7	8	5	1	2	4	2	1	4	3	3
6	3	1	0	2	9	4	7	8	7	1	8	0	2	9

28368	1012434	102089064
029478	2088201	245503834
37020	2092010	839472888843
087478	2789828	2747446705747
186798	05510084	
200405	17403204	
242434	24890248	
432474	38742947	
827859	51041811	

FIND THE NUMBERS

```
4  7  7  4  8  0  3  3  2  0  8  9  1  4  8
7  8  1  0  7  2  9  8  2  7  4  7  4  5  5
2  1  4  8  2  0  6  8  7  2  0  4  1  2  4
6  8  0  9  0  4  3  6  0  3  1  1  0  3  7
3  1  1  5  8  3  3  4  3  2  4  7  8  2  9
8  3  4  4  9  0  3  0  4  8  1  1  6  7  0
0  4  4  4  2  4  2  3  2  2  7  7  5  8  7
3  2  8  4  6  4  1  4  4  0  0  8  6  0  0
9  5  4  9  7  8  9  1  0  1  1  4  8  7  3
0  0  3  8  9  2  4  7  4  7  1  3  8  5  8
3  8  2  2  2  4  8  1  2  5  5  0  1  8  0
3  2  7  4  3  6  9  3  4  0  8  8  7  3  8
3  8  7  4  2  4  7  8  0  0  4  8  6  6  5
4  4  9  3  7  0  1  3  0  8  7  1  7  0  3
9  2  8  7  0  7  0  8  4  3  0  3  4  7  1
```

08948	8031073	8033341107
14027	8075836	14027942418
27018	8402443	14170115847
30348	8742478	14468414073
803903	9499848	54790703808
870708	10685704	74728927018
2034207	803827443	80332089148
5887836	941145887	

FIND THE NUMBERS

```
7  4  9  7  4  8  5  4  2  9  8  1  4  9  5
2  6  0  8  0  4  1  0  2  8  9  4  2  9  4
0  9  5  2  4  4  3  7  8  3  4  1  0  4  8
7  0  0  0  4  7  4  3  8  7  1  0  3  0  9
8  7  1  8  8  8  4  3  6  0  8  3  4  2  2
2  7  2  1  9  3  8  1  8  6  6  3  5  6  4
0  6  9  8  8  3  4  0  8  9  2  5  8  7  7
7  9  2  0  3  7  4  3  7  1  0  8  2  1  9
8  0  5  1  2  1  2  1  7  3  7  2  2  7  4
4  9  8  0  5  8  9  3  0  0  4  4  8  9  2
5  1  1  9  2  1  5  6  8  1  6  9  7  5  6
8  5  7  4  7  8  2  0  1  7  8  0  3  3  3
2  4  6  4  1  4  3  4  7  7  2  1  4  0  2
0  3  3  8  4  2  7  4  6  0  4  9  2  5  2
0  3  5  0  4  7  5  4  7  9  8  4  5  0  0
```

203943	60734380	2783278110
418387	84014387	5489247942
0582097	0218101439	7497485429814
2098344	380634888	
2746049	0548974574	
3871030	747181474	
7088420	857478201	
20782078	2498201408	
039850894	2774341464	

FIND THE NUMBERS

6	2	1	3	3	2	8	9	9	4	7	6	0	5	8
6	6	0	1	0	0	7	3	9	2	4	3	5	2	3
6	6	0	3	7	0	4	0	0	2	4	4	4	6	0
1	4	7	9	3	0	9	7	1	8	4	6	1	5	2
7	4	3	5	8	4	8	9	1	8	4	9	7	8	5
1	9	6	4	0	0	1	2	4	2	4	2	3	5	0
7	0	8	3	7	9	5	1	7	2	8	1	7	5	2
1	8	8	2	4	9	9	8	4	4	0	1	8	0	3
1	5	2	0	0	2	8	0	9	3	9	3	7	2	5
1	6	5	4	6	1	2	4	1	3	8	9	3	0	5
3	1	2	3	9	3	5	7	3	0	0	3	0	0	6
4	2	4	4	0	9	0	4	8	8	8	4	0	8	5
4	8	5	2	1	5	0	2	3	4	2	2	4	5	2
0	8	8	2	0	7	8	9	5	4	3	3	4	1	0
2	1	9	4	7	9	4	1	1	8	3	8	3	1	2

54334	7824990	1708274990
58550	18824998	2033411438
503834	28010990	2834897434
1080630	039850890	5033024990
2015434	50724803	9479411838
6342278	98702880	60718217403
7018418	850674998	

FIND THE NUMBERS

3	3	3	3	8	2	6	4	8	0	2	2	4	8	8
0	1	4	1	8	8	8	4	7	5	2	8	0	3	1
2	4	9	8	1	0	9	8	3	6	6	0	3	4	2
0	7	6	3	8	7	0	9	7	0	3	4	8	4	8
3	7	9	9	3	4	2	4	1	4	8	7	2	0	5
4	5	2	8	5	3	9	8	1	4	5	3	7	2	9
3	1	0	8	2	8	5	4	3	4	1	5	4	0	7
6	4	0	9	5	1	4	8	0	5	8	2	9	8	4
0	2	2	9	4	8	0	2	5	0	2	1	0	7	3
8	8	5	0	3	3	4	5	2	1	4	2	4	9	4
8	9	8	0	5	4	0	1	4	0	8	2	3	1	7
8	0	1	8	4	1	0	9	4	1	4	6	8	2	0
9	9	8	5	4	9	7	4	9	4	8	2	4	4	1
4	8	5	4	7	5	4	2	9	0	7	9	5	7	1
0	2	2	4	5	9	8	2	8	8	9	8	2	2	4

40224	8022488	2498109836
50334	42890982	02784142439
381834	50101408	4598288982
1418414	0184109414	8257488814
5401408	307907836	
5475429	436088894	
6430834	743470114	
7494824	1434582801	

FIND THE NUMBERS

```
2 4 9 9 9 6 5 9 3 9 3 8 5 3 9
7 3 9 4 0 6 3 3 7 8 4 8 1 1 1
2 6 1 0 0 2 3 2 5 6 4 2 8 8 8
4 1 1 6 3 5 2 8 3 1 2 6 1 6 0
1 2 4 6 2 4 7 2 8 3 5 4 4 1 5
5 2 8 7 2 0 8 6 0 1 3 9 5 4 4
1 8 5 9 0 4 2 5 4 7 4 7 5 5 4
3 5 9 4 8 5 3 7 8 3 4 8 6 4 1
6 0 2 6 3 5 8 8 2 3 7 5 7 5 6
2 0 4 0 4 5 4 0 4 7 0 9 4 7 1
6 0 6 4 1 1 2 3 3 7 6 1 9 2 3
7 5 7 5 8 3 1 1 8 0 0 7 3 2 4
9 1 3 3 4 2 4 4 0 3 0 7 1 8 3
5 3 2 2 5 9 0 2 1 8 2 3 7 3 5
8 6 9 0 6 0 4 3 0 2 9 4 5 1 3
```

54702	287208	4254747
146843	470947	06043029
243801	843094	
243847	2898543	

Puzzle #1

HARD

1			4					
		5	7	6		4	3	
						7		
3					5	8		2
				9				
2	1		6					
		8			6			7
								1
					7	3	2	5

Puzzle #2

HARD

	4	6		7			9	3
	9							
1		3					7	
			3		8	5		
7				6				
5		1	4				6	3
				1	2			6
					9			2
			8					

Puzzle #3

HARD

	2	9	7	8				
			4	6			7	
8			2					9
			8					7
	4					6	8	
		3		5				
			9			1	3	
				2		8		
1		5						2

Puzzle #4

HARD

	4			9		6	5	7
			5					
				8	4			
					1			8
				4			9	
7			9	5			2	
3				6		8	7	9
		2			7			1
		6						

Maze 1

Maze 2

Maze 3

Maze 4

Maze 5

Maze 6

Maze 7

Maze 8

Maze 9

Maze 10

Cryptogram Sloth Game Pages

How to Play:

This game is for 1 player

We hope you have fun completing our **cryptograms** games. We have included several of different difficulty levels for you here and the solutions can be found at the end of this section. Enjoy!

IBKLF LK IR ULAN.

_____ __ __ _____.

__ __ ______ __ _ ____?

WDPF LBO FPFQ JBAKFQFK WBJ LBKFNCAR SFRDA?

____ ___ ____ _______ ___ _______ _____?

Cryptograms

1. F RPTMI DTWXR FM F GFQX TZ 6 MT 8 ZXXM GXE DBYAMX.

2. H CKREJ ERKZ OY W HO TRE KHXU, W HO WT YTYVDU
CHSWTD ORZY.

3. K WAIFF WCFM URCWA'U LKHCITWF VTJM CL OATB TU GAKW?
LITWCU

4. BVAFQ WAAWB MKO OUAKRATB, FQON RYZQF HOYZQ TW FA AUO-
FQYKX AE FQO
MUYRMV'B GAXN HOYZQF.

5. OHTYCO DNU QHSXOM TF HDFV PSY DNU KNUDY OLGXXUNO.

6. OUASEO MXD YACOFLDXDL SED RAXUL'O OUARDOS MCFTMU.

7. XVNOLX YIU RNTJG OLINTPLNTO AUJOIYV YDUIFAY YJG JNIOLUIJ
XNTOL YDUIFAY.

8. BHKOZB CPU JKBOHX ZUPMGAKPKNB, MNO KSSCBGKDCHHX BDCSF
KD GDBUSOB.

9. CWUXFC ZAO HV CGSASX ZJSHZW.

10. XELIGX QBC BCEQICF IL QSICQICBX QSF QBNQFJEELX.

11. AFRXWA DRXW BKRFKBO MHRZICJLX IHRQLO AFRXWA XWJX PBHB
JDRQX 12 XR 20
MBBXXJFF.

12. HGRPXH WMU GJCY IL PR 40 SYMFH RGV JU WMLPJCJPS.

13. LYCGML MZOV Z LWUIPCGPS EVYZGPCBLMPF XPGM ZYRZV.

Cryptograms

14. CDNKGC NUDX CDZZJ IPNFK   10 GNFWC I RIX.

____

15. LRANKL LBFHV ZRIALN ZRR AX NKFMU NMIF MH NUFFL.

____

16. ZEQCMZ CMBC YBDWEL XQRWZ B XAZUEW BDW UBEEWI
VMBC?   B
ZEQV   QSS.

____

17. XHPLSX LSNPB BSWL OR BORLJN?   XHPBCWHHX.

____

18. ENLQAE, QABYB PYB EGJ EHBSGBE PMT QABI SLZB GM
QRL
XPYGBQGBE.

____

19. JPQUU-JMUV CEMJPC TQU   TGJSBU SH JPU VTKJSFU.

20. ZBITT-ZPTW ECPZBE HDY ZJIY ZBTAI BTDWE DCGPEZ 360
WTSITTF____
CART DY PVC.

____
21. CTN-CNRQ EZNCDE IFR   VNSCWFVIZ SFRICWFRE.

HINTS

1. M=T	11. R=O
2. Y=E	12. P=T
3. T=I	13. P=I
4. O=E	14. C=S
5. D=A	15. L=S
6. D=E	16. W=E
7. I=R	17. L=T
8. K=O	18. E=S
9. S=I	19. J=T
10. C=E	20. Z=T
	21. R=E

ANSWERS

1. A sloth moves at a pace of 6 to 8 feet per   minute.

2. A sloth told me I am not lazy, I am in energy saving mode.

3. A three toed sloth's favorite kind of chip is what? Fritos

4. Sloth poops are enormous, they might weigh up to one-third of the animal's body weight.

5. Sloths are clumsy on land but are great swimmers.

6. Sloths are considered the world's slowest animal.

7. Sloths are found throughout Central America and northern South America.

8. Sloths are mostly herbivorous, but occasionally snack on insects.

9. Sloths are my spirit   animal.

10. Sloths are related to anteaters and armadillos.

ANSWERS

11. Sloths both evolved from giant ground sloths that were about 12 to 20 feet tall.

12. Sloths can live up to 40 years old in captivity.

13. Sloths have a symbiotic relationship with algae.

14. Sloths only sleep about 10 hours a day.

15. Sloths spend almost all of their time in trees.

16. Sloths that barely moves a muscle are called what? A slow off.

17. Sloths throw what in winter? Slowballs.

18. Sloths, there are six species and they come in two varieties.

19. Three-toed sloths are active in the daytime.

20. Three-toed sloths can turn their heads almost 360 degrees like an owl.

21. Two-toed sloths are nocturnal creatures.

Solutions

1.Trivia

1. What is Bob Dylan's real name?

    Robert Zimmerman

2. Johnny Depp is famously afraid of what?

    Clowns

3. Caesar salad originated from which country?

    Mexico

4. Who wrote Flowers for Algernon?

    Daniel Keyes

5. What did Spain introduce to Ireland in the late 1500s?

    Potatoes

6. Which famous landmark is visible from space?

    The Great Pyramids at Giza

7. What is the smallest country in the world?

    Vatican City

8. In 1917 Finland declared its independence from which country?

    Russia

9. The Paris Peace Accords ended which conflict?

   Vietnam War

10. Which country is the least populated?

    Vatican City

11. What is the main ingredient of Bombay Duck?

    Fish

12. DNA is arranged into structures known as what?

    Chromosomes

13. Which city was Beethoven born in?

    Bonn

14. What is the only king in a deck of cards without a moustache?

    King of hearts

15. Where might you keep bees?

    Apiary

16. In what year did Neil Armstrong land on the moon?

    1969

17. What year did Queen Victoria become Queen?

1837

18. What happened in the Soviet Union from 1933-1934?

Famine

19. What is the capital of Qatar?

Doha

20. What year did Harriet Tubman escape slavery?

1849

21. Marilyn Monroe was married to which famous sportsman?

Joe DiMaggio

22. Which New York Yankee player was nicknamed the "Yankee Clipper"?

Joe DiMaggio

23. Which gas makes up 91% of the sun?

Hydrogen

24. What is the longest mountain range in the world?

Andes

25. Which instrument is associated with Earl Bud Powell?

   Piano

26. What christian denomination was founded by John Wesley in 1738?

   Methodist

27. In what month does Russia celebrate the October Revolution?

   November

28. Which US city is known as the City of Brotherly

   Philadelphia

29. Which country is the oldest?

   Portugal

30. Which country produces the most coffee in the world?

   Brazil

31. Julius Caesar was kidnapped by who in 78 BC?

   pirates

32. How old was King Tut when he died?

   19

33. In June in Wyoming it is illegal to take a picture of what?

A rabbit

34. Where did Rene Descartes spend the last year of his life?

Sweden

35. In what country would one compete in a wife carry race?

Finland

36. The Ring of Fire is located in which ocean?

Pacific

37. Where is the Easter Island located?

Chile

38. Name the team with the most Super Bowl appearances?

New England Patriots

39. Which of the following is not a computer coding language?

Snake

40. What is the name of Donald Duck's sister?

Della Duck

41. Which of Shakespeare's plays is the longest?

Hamlet

42. What igneous rock has a density less than water?

Pumice

43. Which U.S. President was the first to hold a Patent?

Lincoln

44. What does a pteridologist study?

Ferns

45. Which Dutch artist painted Girl with a Pearl Earring?

Vermeer

46. The oldest living person lived in which country?

France

47. Who was the first tsar of Russia?

Ivan IV

48. How many times was Dr. Seuss's first book rejected?

27

49. What planets literally rain diamonds?

Saturn and Jupiter

50. What year did women get the right to vote in the U.S?

1920

2.Word search

Puzzle # 1
ASSORTED WORDS 1

S	E	C	O	N	D	H	A	N	D			
	S	E	R	G	E			M				
A		C			N		B	L	U	S	H	E	R
	X	O			E	V	I	T	N	E	T	E	R
G	N	I	T	A	U	T	C	E	F	F	E	C
U		F	O		S	U	O	N	E	V	A	R	I
Z		F	M		G	D		C				D
Z	S	I		A		N	E	J	M
L	T	N	S	P	A	T	E	S	I	T	O	E
E	U	G		S	F	E	I	H	C	K	F	I
R	M			F	L	I	C	K	E	R	I	N	G
	P	D	E	H	S	I	D	N	A	R	B	A	R	S
	I	D	E	Z	E	P	A	R	T	L		L
U	N	A	D	O	R	N	E	D			L
	G	S	H	I	M	M	I	E	S			Y

Puzzle # 2
ASSORTED WORDS 2

S	F	R	A	N	C	H	I	S	E	D	C
S		T			E	S	A	B	E	E	R	F
R	N	T	N	A	R	C	H	D	E	A	C	O	N
	E	O	N	E	T	B			D		S
S	R	G	U	I	A	M	S	A		V		S	P
	N	E	R	S	T	N	Y	I	R		O		R	U
F	S	O	S	A	C	U	G	O	E	G	C		O	S
M	F	G	I	S	D	E	B	I	L	H	A		A	H
Y	U	O	N	S	O	U	R	I	L	P	T	I	D	E
U	M	S	W	I	R	R	A	V	R	A	E	N	N	R
K	B		C	O	L	E	C	T	I	T	M	D	A	S
K	L			L	H	B	V		I	C	T	N		P
I	E			E	S	M	R		O	A	A	O
N	D				D		U	E		N	L		N
G			P	I	L	L	S		B	P		S

Puzzle # 3
ASSORTED WORDS 3

			I	R	R	I	G	A	T	E	S		S
P	O	V	E	R	D	R	E	S	S	I	N	G		P
R	R	L	Y	R	I	C	S	W	C				E
E	E		M	U	C			E	O				E
C	E		E	S	N	A		N	L				D
A	L		M		D	M	M		F	I	G		R	B
U	I		O		A	A	U	I		B		U	O
T	N	O	I	T	C	A	R	T	S	I	D	R	N	A
I	G	S	R	I	P	A	T	G	C			A	T
O	F	F	S	P	R	I	N	G	A	H		W	C
N				F	L	A	T	B	E	D	A
S	S	T	N	E	M	A	M	R	I	F		D	Y
		I	N	T	E	R	P	O	S	E	S
			Y	R	O	T	A	N	I	M
M	O	U	N	T	A	I	N	T	O	P	S

Puzzle # 4
ASSORTED WORDS 4

		G	P	Y	H	T	I	W	E	R	E	H
	I		S	N	R	L	O
S	S	M	R	N	I	O	L	N					R
	A	R	I	A	A	H	F	A	E				E
	S	T	O	S	D	M	C	F	R	S			D
	E	C	T	S	I	O	T	E	E	T			U
	T	H	A	I	U	T	O	R	D	L			C
		A	E	R	N	S	T	L	E	E	Y	T
		M	L	R	A	E	O	B	D	F	I
B	O	U	I	L	L	A	B	A	I	S	S	E		O
L	I	K	E	N	E	D	G		N	P				N
D	I	P	R	O	T		L	L	A	B	T	O	O	F
		I	D	I	O	M	A	T	I	C
			G	N	I	P	M	I	R	C
T	R	A	C	H	E	A	S	O	A	C	A	C

Puzzle # 5
ASSORTED WORDS 5

```
A D M O N I S H M E N T S S
  E   G       C           O H S
  S   N G N O T I C E D L O Q
P E   N N I C   N       V V U
E R   G G A I K L   I     E E E
R V   T L F P N A O     L   L E
S I   A E O   D E M G     C I Z
U C   X A L R   A T H S     N E
A E S I M L   Y   E S C     G R
S A Q I S I       D I T       S
I B U N D E R A R F N I O A
O L A G   S P S T O K E S M M
N E W P A R B O I L S
    S E Z I R A L O P
        N E M Y R E S R U N
```

Puzzle # 6
ASSORTED WORDS 6

```
Y S P E L A T A C         C   P
  N D E V I S U L L I     A   E
F L O O R E C O R D E D N L   R
    U G N I K L I M       N U S
    C L A R B I T R A T O R E
R J H   O W   Y       D N I V
E E I S   O A   L       O B D E
S V N G E   S D B I     G A N R
U I G   S R   E I   M F L E A
M L S     A O   N E   O L S N
I D   Y     W C N S S U O S C
N O   A L M A N A C S G   L E
G E     A       C B   H   G
  R       N   L   L T
  S         A E     A
```

Puzzle # 7
ASSORTED WORDS 7

```
  D     E S F L O R I D L Y C
    E C   C U         I N R
I   M P E   N O       M O O
M     A P L D A U     B N S
P     B U I L E D N   E P S
E T S E I L R U B R I   R L W
      R I T L U O T S U A
C   T     C N   O N C N S L
E     P     H G   I K N O K
P     M P I C K E R D I O C
T C O M M E M O R A T E S N C
I S T N E M T S I L N E     G
B         S T E N G A M
L S E S S O R T A B L A
E R E H C N U P W O C
```

Puzzle # 8
ASSORTED WORDS 8

```
        D H O B B L I N G
N   D   D I P O L E
  O M E L B M E T S E L B O N
  B I   X   S E D E
    L T Y O   G T N O
A R M O R S M P N A E F
D     O O S M R I M C
  E       D B E U O L I S
    N     S A M L M S T E
      E       H I   F O I L D
        E       O T   T U U
  S E S U R E V O T N     E Q
Y G D U P W A F F U G A     R
  G N I S O L C E R O F
    F R A N C H I S E E S
```

Puzzle # 5
ASSORTED WORDS 5

A	D	M	O	N	I	S	H	M	E	N	T	S	S	
		E		G			C					O	H	S
	S		N	G	N	O	T	I	C	E	D	L	O	Q
P	E			N	N	I	C		N			V	V	U
E	R		G	G	A	I	K	L		I		E	E	E
R	V		T	L	F	P	N	A	O		L		L	E
S	I		A	E	O		D	E	M	G		C	I	Z
U	C		X	A	L	R		A	T	H	S		N	E
A	E	S	I	M	L		Y	E	S	C			G	R
S	A	Q	I	S	I				D	I	T			S
I	B	U	N	D	E	R	A	R	F	N	I	O	A	
O	L	A	G		S	P	S	T	O	K	E	S	M	M
N	E	W	P	A	R	B	O	I	L	S				
	S	E	Z	I	R	A	L	O	P					
		N	E	M	Y	R	E	S	R	U	N			

Puzzle # 6
ASSORTED WORDS 6

Y	S	P	E	L	A	T	A	C				C		P
	N	D	E	V	I	S	U	L	L	I		A		E
F	L	O	O	R	E	C	O	R	D	E	D	N	L	R
		U	G	N	I	K	L	I	M			N	U	S
		C	L	A	R	B	I	T	R	A	T	O	R	E
R	J	H			O	W		Y			D	N	I	V
E	E	I	S			O	A		L		O	B	D	E
S	V	N	G	E			S	D	B	I	G	A	N	R
U	I	G			S	R		E	I	M	F	L	E	A
M	L	S				A	O		N	E	O	L	S	N
I	D			Y		W	C	N	S	S	U	O	S	C
N	O		A	L	M	A	N	A	C	S	G		L	E
G	E					A			C	B	H			G
	R						N		L	L	T			
	S						A	E			A			

3.Circle Maze

Maze
#1

Maze
#2

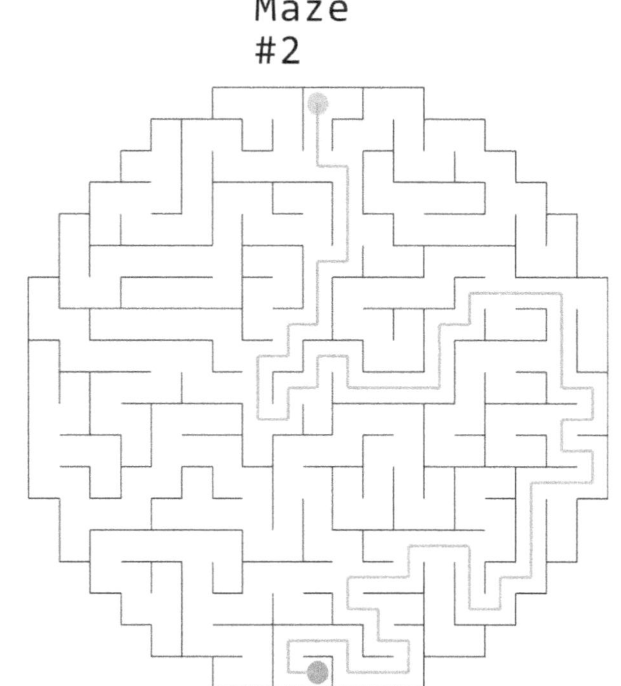

Maze
#3

Maze
#4

Maze
#5

Maze
#6

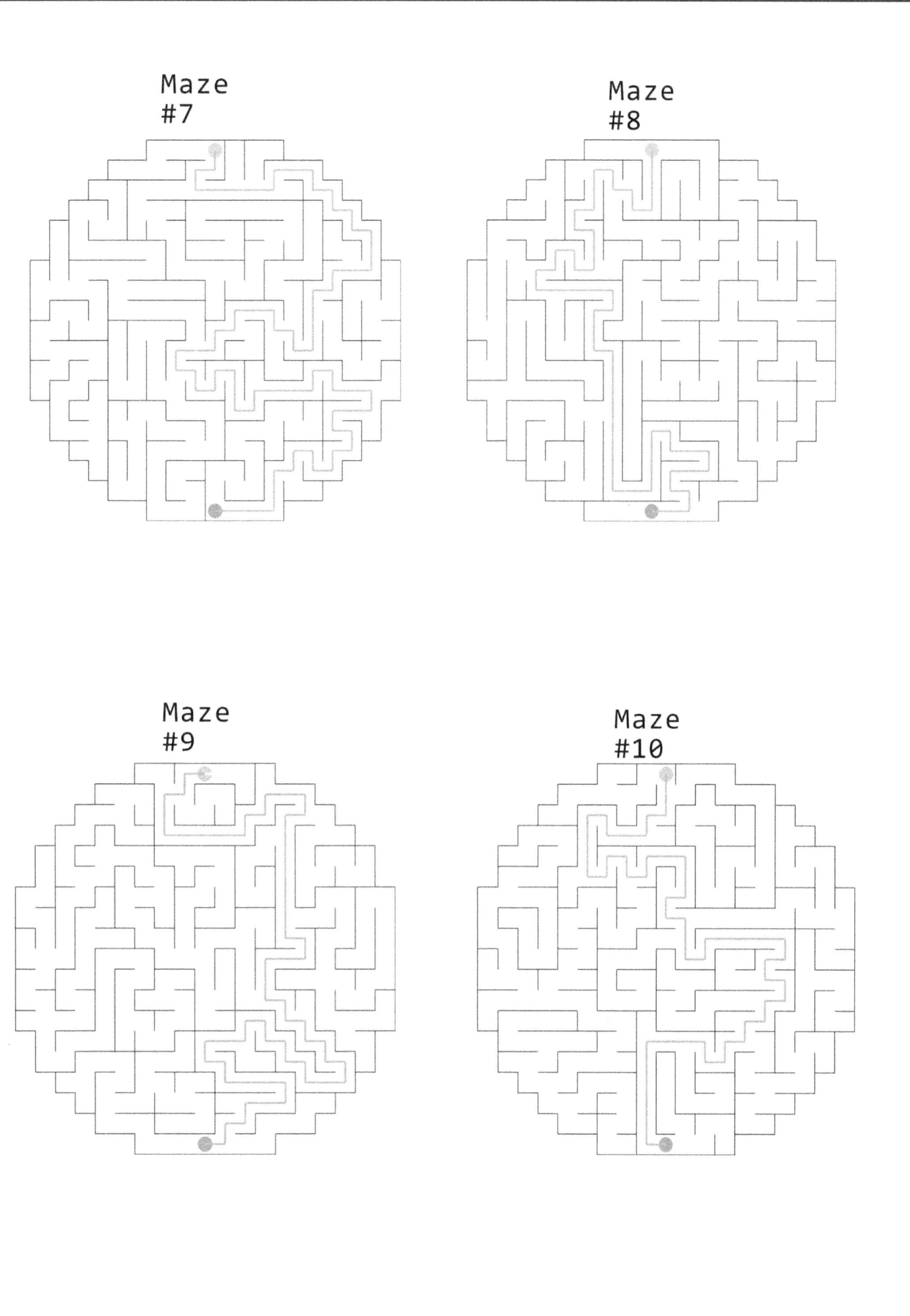

Maze
#7
Maze
#8
Maze
#9
Maze
#10

4.Find The Numbers

FIND THE NUMBERS
Puzzle # 1

	4			1	8	9	9	1	4	7	4	2	0	8
		3	6			3			7					3
3		0	0	3	0		1	5	8	4	7	7	4	3
	4	3	3	1	8	0		4			1			8
		9	7	3	0	8	4	3	2		1	4		0
4		3	8	4	0	1	3	3	8	3	4	2	3	3
	3		4	4	2	5	0	0	0	9	8	4		0
7	5	8	0	8	1	3	4	4	1	9	8	1		5
4	7	3	4	8	0	7	4	1	5	1	4	0	8	4
3	4	4	4	2	1	2	0	2	8	4		2	0	1
4	4	5	1	3	8	2	0	7		8	2	1	1	8
1	3	0		4	1	4	0	9	2	9		0	4	8
0	8	8			3	4	3	1		4		8	2	
1	3	9			2	0	7	8	4	3	2	8	9	4
0	9	4	5	5	4	7	8	4	3	2	8	9	4	

FIND THE NUMBERS
Puzzle # 2

		3	4	8	9	0	2	2	0	1	5	3	8	
						8	5	1	8	3	9			
7	3	8	9				4							
	4	2	2	3		8		7						
	0	1	7	2	0		9		2					
	7		4	8	0	9		8		9				
	4			5	1	3	2		9		0			
	1	1				3	4	4		2		7		
	4	1				1	1	5		7		2		
	6	0	3	2	8	8	8	8	4	3		4		
	4	3						7	6	8		8		
		0							9	4	8			
	4	7	8	0	7	2	1	4	4	7	2	8		
		9												3
		4	5	0	7	4	7	9	4	8	8	4	7	5

FIND THE NUMBERS
Puzzle # 3

							7	6						
		1	0	3	7	4	1	4	3					
		6	3	8	3	4	4	5	1	8				
8							2	1	1	8	9	9	1	4
	1		1	4	8	4	2	4		4	3	8		
	2	3		0			0	8		2	6	4		
	0	7	1		0	3		1		0		7		
		1	4	1	8	4	1	8	3	6	8		8	
8	7	0	7	4	4	3	7	3	3		3		1	
		7		0	6		3			6	4			
			0			0		4			7			
			2			4		8			8			
	9	4	3	3	4	7	3	4	8	8	7		9	
		4	1	1	4	4	5		8		7			
													9	

FIND THE NUMBERS
Puzzle # 4

		0	7	0	0	2	7	0	2	0	7	4	5	
3	8	8	8	0	3	0	0	0	7	1	0	2		
8				3	1	0	9	7	8	0	7	0	0	
9	3	0	9	1	0	7	2	2	0	1	0	1	0	
5	4	4	8			2	4	3	3	8	0	1	0	
0		0	3	0	0	7	3	0	7	2		0	4	2
2		0	2			0		0			0	2	4	7
3		7	7	7		4	3	4	2	0	3	0	1	8
0		0	4	6	0	0	3	0	2	7	0	1	7	2
		0	1		8	0					0	8	0	2
1	8	7	2	3	8	0	7	0					3	7
	7	2	0	5	7	0	0	8	3	9	0	1	0	0
		0	1	0	6	7	4	2	3	0	4	2	1	3
				4	3	0	1	0	7	0			0	
1	0	2	3	4	2	3	0	2	0	0			0	

FIND THE NUMBERS
Puzzle # 5

2	4	5	5	0	3	8	3	4	8	6	3	8	2	4
3	4	8	8	8	8	2	7	4	9	3	8			5
	7	4	7	5	0	7	6	4	4	7	4	7	2	4
			6	4	1	0	0	0	4	7	1	1	7	3
			4	0	2	3	0	4	7	1		8	8	8
5				5	9			2				6	9	3
1	8			5		8	7		0			7	8	6
0	0	4	1	1			0	4	4	7		9	2	3
4	2	2	2	0		2		2	9	7	3	8	8	8
1		0	8	0	1	9	0	4	0	2	4			6
8			0	8	9	2	5	9	3	1	4	2		7
1			4	0	8	4	8	2	4			7	3	9
1				0	2	4	3	7	0	2			8	4
0	8	7	4	7	8	5		2	4	2	1	4		3
			0	2	9	4	7	8				8	0	2

FIND THE NUMBERS
Puzzle # 6

		7		8	0	3	3	2	0	8	9	1	4	8
	8	1	0	7	2	9	8	2	7	4	7			5
		4	8	2				7	2	0	4	1		4
	8		9	0	4	3	6			1	1			7
	1	1		8	3	3	4	3		4		8		9
8	3	4	4	9	0	3	0	4	8	1				0
0	4	4	4	2	4		3	2	2	7			8	7
3		8	4	6	4	1	4	4		0	8		0	0
9			9	7	8	9	1	0	1	1	4	8	7	3
0				9	2	4	7	4	7	1		8	5	8
3					4	8	1	2	5	5	0		8	0
						9	3	4	0	8	8	7	3	8
	8	7	4	2	4	7	8	0	0	4	8	6	6	
			3	7	0	1	3	0	8	7	1	7	0	
		8	7	0	7	0	8	4	3	0	3			1

FIND THE NUMBERS
Puzzle # 7

7	4	9	7	4	8	5	4	2	9	8	1	4		5
2		0	8	0	4	1	0	2	8	9	4	2		4
0			2	4	4		7	8	3	4	1	0	4	8
7	0		0	4	7	4	3	8	7	1	0	3	0	9
8		1	8	8	8	4	3	6	0	8	3			2
2	7		1	9	3	8	1	8			3			4
0		9		8	3	4	0	8	9			8		7
7			0		7	4	3	7	1	0			1	9
8				2		2	1	7	3	7	2			4
4	9	8	0	5	8	9	3	0	0	4	4			2
						5		8	1	6	9	7		
8	5	7	4	7	8	2	0	1	7	8		3		
	4	6	4	1	4	3	4	7	7	2	1		0	
					2	7	4	6	0	4	9	2		2
				4	7	5	4	7	9	8	4	5	0	

FIND THE NUMBERS
Puzzle # 8

	2			3		8	9	9	4	7	6	0	5	8
		0	1		0	7	3							
		0	3	7	0	4	0	0						
	4		9	3	0	9	7	1	8				5	
		3		8	4	8	9	1	8	4			8	
1		6	4	0	0	1	2	4	2	4	2		5	
7	0		3	7	9	5	1	7	2	8	1	7	5	
1	8	8	2	4	9	9	8	4	4	0	1	8	0	
		2	0	0	2	8	0	9	3	9	3	7		5
			4	6	1	2	4	1	3	8	9	3	0	
				9	3	5	7	3	0	0	3	0	0	6
				9	0	4	8	8	8			0		5
					0		3			2	2		5	
0	8	8	2	0	7	8	9	5	4	3	3	4		
		9	4	7	9	4	1	1	8	3	8			

FIND THE NUMBERS
Puzzle # 9

					6		8	0	2	2	4	8	8	
		4	1	8	8	8	4	7	5	2	8			
2	4	9	8	1	0	9	8	3	6					
		6	3	8	7	0	9	7	0	3				
			9	3	4	2	4	1	4	8	7	2	0	
4					3		1			3				
3	1	0	8	2	8	5	4	3	4	1		4		7
6	4				1	4			5	8				4
0	2				8		2		0		1			3
8	8	5	0	3	3	4		2	1			4		4
8	9			5	4	0	1	4	0	8			1	7
8	0	1	8	4	1	0	9	4	1	4				0
9	9					7	4	9	4	8	2	4		1
4	8	5	4	7	5	4	2	9	0					1
	2		4	5	9	8	2	8	8	9	8	2		4

FIND THE NUMBERS
Puzzle # 10

	4													
		9												
			0											
				3										
2			4		2									
2	8	7	2	0	8		0							
	9		4	2	5	4	7	4	7					
	8		3						3	4	8	6	4	1
		5		8	2				5					
		4					4	7	0	9	4	7		
								3	3	7				
								8						
								0						
								1						
	0	6	0	4	3	0	2	9						

5.Hard Sudoku

Puzzle # 1

1	7	6	4	3	8	2	5	9
9	2	5	7	6	1	4	3	8
4	8	3	5	2	9	7	1	6
3	6	4	1	7	5	8	9	2
8	5	7	3	9	2	1	6	4
2	1	9	6	8	4	5	7	3
5	3	8	2	1	6	9	4	7
7	4	2	9	5	3	6	8	1
6	9	1	8	4	7	3	2	5

Puzzle # 2

8	4	6	2	7	5	1	9	3
2	9	7	1	3	6	4	8	5
1	5	3	9	8	4	2	7	6
4	6	9	3	2	8	5	1	7
7	3	8	5	6	1	9	4	2
5	2	1	4	9	7	6	3	8
9	8	5	7	1	2	3	6	4
3	7	4	6	5	9	8	2	1
6	1	2	8	4	3	7	5	9

Puzzle # 3

6	2	9	7	8	5	4	1	3
3	5	1	4	6	9	2	7	8
8	7	4	2	1	3	5	6	9
9	1	6	8	4	2	3	5	7
5	4	2	3	9	7	6	8	1
7	8	3	1	5	6	9	2	4
2	6	8	9	7	4	1	3	5
4	3	7	5	2	1	8	9	6
1	9	5	6	3	8	7	4	2

Puzzle # 4

8	4	3	1	9	2	6	5	7
1	2	9	5	7	6	3	8	4
6	5	7	3	8	4	9	1	2
4	9	5	6	2	1	7	3	8
2	6	8	7	4	3	1	9	5
7	3	1	9	5	8	4	2	6
3	1	4	2	6	5	8	7	9
9	8	2	4	3	7	5	6	1
5	7	6	8	1	9	2	4	3

6.Hard Maze

Maze 1

Maze 2

Maze 3

Maze 4

Maze 5

Maze 6

Maze 7

Maze 8

Maze 9

Maze 10

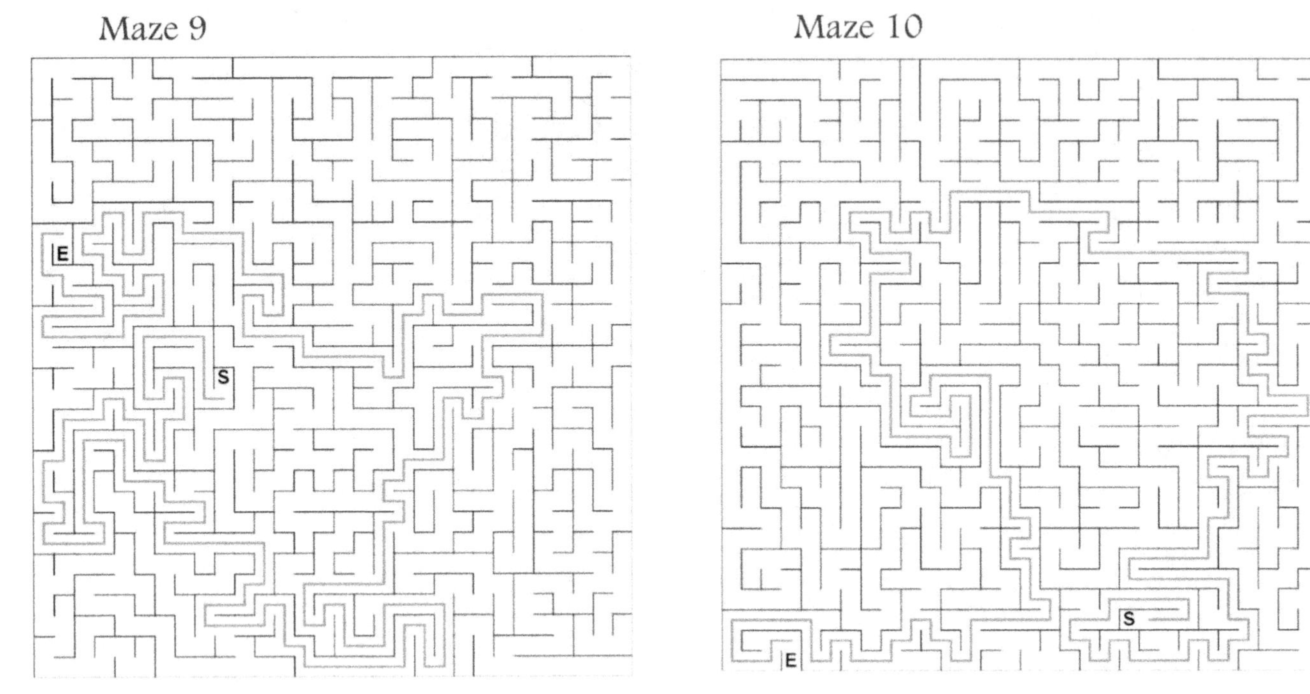

7.Cryptogram

ANSWERS

1. A sloth moves at a pace of 6 to 8 feet per   minute.

2. A sloth told me I am not lazy, I am in energy saving mode.

3. A three toed sloth's favorite kind of chip is what? Fritos

4. Sloth poops are enormous, they might weigh up to one-third of the
animal's body weight.

5. Sloths are clumsy on land but are great swimmers.

6. Sloths are considered the world's slowest animal.

7. Sloths are found throughout Central America and northern South
America.

8. Sloths are mostly herbivorous, but occasionally snack on insects.

9. Sloths are my spirit   animal.

10. Sloths are related to anteaters and armadillos.

ANSWERS

11. Sloths both evolved from giant ground sloths that were about 12 to 20 feet tall.

12. Sloths can live up to 40 years old in captivity.

13. Sloths have a symbiotic relationship with algae.

14. Sloths only sleep about   10 hours a day.

15. Sloths spend almost all of their time in trees.

16. Sloths that barely moves a muscle are called what? A slow off.

17. Sloths throw what in   winter? Slowballs.

18. Sloths, there are six species and they come in two varieties.

19. Three-toed sloths are   active in the daytime.

20. Three-toed sloths can turn their heads almost 360 degrees like an owl.

21. Two-toed sloths are   nocturnal creatures.

I want to thank
You for purchasing
This Book. I would
be very grateful for
taking a moment
and leaving
feedback. It helps
our small business
grow and reach
more people.